PALEO SMOOTHIES

Publications International, Ltd.

Louis Weber, CEO
Publications International, Ltd.
7373 North Cicero Avenue
Lincolnwood, IL 60712

Permission is never granted for commercial purposes.

Photography on pages 5, 7, 11, 13, 21, 23, 29, 31, 33, 37, 41, 45, 47, 49, 51, 53, 57, 59, 63, 71, 73, 75, 91, 95, 97, 99, 101, 103, 109, 113, 115, 117, 121, 123, 125, 127, 129, 133, 137, 139, 141, 143, 145, 147, 151 153, 155, 159, 163, 165, 167, 169, 173, 175, 179, 181, 183 and 185 by PIL Photo Studio North.

Pictured on the front cover *(left to right):* Papaya-Pineapple Smoothie *(page 82),* Refresh Smoothie *(page 160)* and Green Islander Smoothie *(page 66).*

Pictured on the back cover *(left to right):* Blueberry Apple Booster *(page 128),* Cantaloupe Strawberry Sunrise *(page 10)* and Raspberry Pear Refresher *(page 168).*

ISBN: 978-1-4508-9989-5

Library of Congress Control Number: 2014958605

Manufactured in China.

8 7 6 5 4 3 2 1

Publications International, Ltd.

TABLE OF CONTENTS

BREAKFAST BLENDS

JUST PEACHY CANTALOUPE SMOOTHIE
Makes 2 servings

¼ cup orange juice

2 cups frozen sliced peaches

1½ cups cantaloupe chunks

1 tablespoon almond butter

Combine orange juice, peaches, cantaloupe and almond butter in blender; blend until smooth. Serve immediately.

BANANA CHAI SMOOTHIE

Makes 2 servings

¾ cup water

¼ cup unsweetened coconut milk

2 frozen bananas

1 teaspoon honey

¼ teaspoon ground ginger

¼ teaspoon ground cinnamon

¼ teaspoon vanilla

Pinch ground cloves (optional)

Combine water, coconut milk, bananas, honey, ginger, cinnamon, vanilla and cloves, if desired, in blender; blend until smooth. Serve immediately.

MANGO CITRUS SMOOTHIE

Makes 2 servings

2 tangerines

1 cup frozen mango chunks

¼ cup ice cubes

Juice of 1 lime

1 tablespoon honey

1. Grate peel from tangerines; peel and seed tangerines.

2. Combine tangerine sections and grated peel in blender with mango, ice, lime juice and honey; blend until smooth. Serve immediately.

CANTALOUPE STRAWBERRY SUNRISE >

Makes 2 servings

1 cup cantaloupe chunks

2 clementines, peeled

1 cup frozen strawberries

Combine cantaloupe, clementines and strawberries in blender; blend until smooth. Serve immediately.

HONEYDEW GINGER SMOOTHIE

Makes 1 serving

1 cup honeydew chunks

½ cup frozen banana slices

2 tablespoons water

½ teaspoon grated fresh ginger

Combine honeydew, banana, water and ginger in blender; blend until smooth. Serve immediately.

QUADRUPLE ORANGE SMOOTHIE

Makes 2 servings

½ **cup water**

3 **medium carrots, peeled and cut into chunks (about 6 ounces)**

1 **navel orange, peeled and seeded**

1 **clementine, peeled**

½ **cup frozen mango chunks**

Combine water, carrots, orange, clementine and mango in blender; blend until smooth. Serve immediately.

BREAKFAST POM SMOOTHIE

Makes 2 servings

¾ cup pomegranate juice

½ cup unsweetened almond milk

 1 frozen banana

½ cup sliced fresh strawberries

½ cup fresh blueberries

Combine pomegranate juice, almond milk, banana, strawberries and blueberries in blender; blend until smooth. Serve immediately.

CREAMY STRAWBERRY-BANANA SHAKE

Makes 3 servings

¾ **cup orange juice**

2¼ **cups ice cubes**

1 **banana**

¾ **cup fresh strawberries, hulled**

½ **avocado, pitted and peeled**

Combine orange juice, ice, banana, strawberries and avocado in blender; blend until smooth. Serve immediately.

MANGO MADNESS

Makes 2 servings

½ **cup unsweetened almond milk**

¼ **cup water**

¼ **cup orange juice**

 1 **cup frozen mango chunks**

½ **cup frozen sliced peaches**

½ **banana**

Combine almond milk, water, orange juice mango, peaches and banana in blender; blend until smooth. Serve immediately.

CREAMY CHOCOLATE SMOOTHIE >

Makes 1 serving

1 cup unsweetened almond milk

1 frozen banana

½ avocado, pitted and peeled

1 tablespoon honey

1 tablespoon unsweetened cocoa powder

Combine almond milk, banana, avocado, honey and cocoa in blender; blend until smooth. Serve immediately.

TROPICAL BREAKFAST SMOOTHIE

Makes 2 servings

¼ cup orange juice

1 cup fresh pineapple chunks

½ banana

¼ cup ice cubes

2 tablespoons flaked coconut

½ tablespoon lime juice

Combine orange juice, pineapple, banana, ice, coconut and lime juice in blender; blend until smooth. Serve immediately.

MORNING GLORY SMOOTHIE

Makes 2 servings

1 pink or ruby red grapefruit, peeled, seeded and pith removed

1 banana

¾ cup frozen strawberries

1 teaspoon honey

Combine grapefruit, banana, strawberries and honey in blender; blend until smooth. Serve immediately.

BANANA-PINEAPPLE BREAKFAST SHAKE

Makes 2 servings

½ **cup unsweetened almond milk**

1 **cup fresh pineapple chunks**

1 **frozen banana**

½ **cup ice cubes**

1 **teaspoon vanilla**

⅛ **teaspoon ground nutmeg**

Combine almond milk, pineapple, banana, ice, vanilla and nutmeg in blender; blend until smooth. Serve immediately.

STRAWBERRY MANGO SMOOTHIE
Makes 3 servings

¾ **cup apricot juice**

2 **cups fresh strawberries, hulled**

1 **cup frozen mango chunks**

¼ **cup ice cubes**

Combine apricot juice, strawberries, mango and ice in blender; blend until smooth.
Serve immediately.

FRUIT FAVORITES

....

ORCHARD MEDLEY

Makes 3 servings

½ cup water

2 plums, pitted and cut into chunks

1 sweet red apple, seeded and cut into chunks

1 pear, seeded and cut into chunks

2 teaspoons lemon juice

Combine water, plums, apple, pear and lemon juice in blender; blend until smooth. Serve immediately.

RUBY RED DELIGHT

Makes 2 servings

¼ cup water

1 navel orange, peeled and seeded

1 medium beet, peeled and cut into chunks

½ cup seedless red grapes

½ cup frozen strawberries

¼ teaspoon ground ginger

Combine water, orange, beet, grapes, strawberries and ginger in blender; blend until smooth. Serve immediately.

CARROT CAKE SMOOTHIE

Makes 1 serving

½ **cup coconut water**

3 **medium carrots, peeled and cut into chunks (about 6 ounces)**

½ **banana**

½ **cup frozen pineapple chunks**

1 **teaspoon honey**

⅛ **teaspoon ground cinnamon**

⅛ **teaspoon ground ginger**

Combine coconut water, carrots, banana, pineapple, honey, cinnamon and ginger in blender; blend until smooth. Serve immediately.

CANTALOUPE SMOOTHIE >

Makes 1 serving

½ **orange juice**

2 **cups cantaloupe chunks**

½ **cup ice cubes**

½ **teaspoon vanilla**

Combine orange juice, cantaloupe, ice and vanilla in blender; blend until smooth. Serve immediately.

TANGERAPPLE SMOOTHIE

Makes 1 serving

1 **sweet red apple, seeded and cut into chunks**

1 **tangerine, peeled and seeded**

1 **frozen banana**

Combine apple, tangerine and banana in blender; blend until smooth. Serve immediately.

GREAT GRAPE ESCAPE

Makes 2 servings

¼ cup water

1 tangerine, peeled and seeded

1 cup frozen seedless red grapes

½ cup frozen raspberries

1 teaspoon lemon juice

Combine water, tangerine, grapes, raspberries and lemon juice in blender; blend until smooth. Serve immediately.

CHERRY COOLER

Makes 3 servings

3 cups orange juice

8 ounces fresh cherries, pitted

½ teaspoon vanilla

½ cup ice cubes

Combine orange juice, cherries, vanilla and ice in blender; blend until smooth. Serve immediately.

SWEET SPINACH SENSATION

Makes 2 servings

½ cup water

1 sweet red apple, seeded and cut into chunks

1 tangerine, peeled and seeded

1 cup frozen mango chunks

1 cup baby spinach

Combine water, apple, tangerine, mango and spinach in blender; blend until smooth. Serve immediately.

KIWI STRAWBERRY SMOOTHIE >

Makes 3 servings

1½ cups unsweetened coconut milk

3 kiwis, peeled and quartered

1½ cups sliced fresh strawberries

¾ cup ice cubes

1½ tablespoons honey

Combine coconut milk, kiwis, strawberries, ice and honey in blender; blend until smooth. Serve immediately.

EASY APPLE PIE SMOOTHIE

Makes 1 serving

½ cup water

1 sweet red apple, seeded and cut into chunks

1 tablespoon honey

¼ teaspoon ground cinnamon

¼ teaspoon vanilla

Pinch each ground allspice and ground nutmeg

Combine water, apple, honey, cinnamon, vanilla, allspice and nutmeg in blender; blend until smooth. Serve immediately.

PURPLE PLEASER SMOOTHIE

Makes 3 servings

½ cup water

2 cups seedless red grapes

2 cups frozen blackberries

2 cups baby spinach

½ cup ice cubes

¼ teaspoon ground cinnamon

Combine water, grapes, blackberries, spinach, ice and cinnamon in blender; blend until smooth. Serve immediately.

PEACH APRICOT PARADISE

Makes 2 servings

½ **cup dried apricots**

¼ **cup water**

¼ **cup orange juice**

1 **cup frozen sliced peaches**

¼ **teaspoon ground ginger**

1. Place apricots in small bowl; cover with hot water. Let stand 10 minutes or until soft; drain.

2. Combine ¼ cup water, orange juice, peaches, apricots and ginger in blender; blend until smooth. Serve immediately.

STRAWBERRY APPLE SMOOTHIE

Makes 2 servings

¾ cup water

1 sweet red apple, seeded and cut into chunks

1 clementine, peeled

1 cup frozen strawberries

1 tablespoon lemon juice

Combine water, apple, clementine, strawberries and lemon juice in blender; blend until smooth. Serve immediately.

GOING GREEN

....

TRIPLE GREEN SMOOTHIE

Makes 2 servings

2 cups green grapes

1 kiwi, peeled and quartered

½ avocado, pitted and peeled

Combine grapes, kiwi and avocado in blender; blend until smooth. Serve immediately.

SPINACH APPLE SATISFACTION

Makes 1 serving

¼ **cup apple juice**

1 **Granny Smith apple, seeded and cut into chunks**

1 **cup baby spinach**

½ **cup ice**

½ **avocado, pitted and peeled**

1 **teaspoon almond butter**

½ **teaspoon grated fresh ginger**

Combine apple juice, apple, spinach, ice, avocado, almond butter and ginger in blender; blend until smooth. Serve immediately.

TROPICAL GREEN SHAKE

Makes 3 servings

¾ **cup orange juice**

1½ **cups packed stemmed kale**

1½ **cups frozen tropical fruit mix***

1½ **cups ice cubes**

3 **tablespoons honey**

*Tropical mix typically contains pineapple, mango and strawberries along with other fruit.

Combine orange juice, kale, tropical fruit mix, ice and honey in blender; blend until smooth. Serve immediately.

SWEET GREEN SUPREME

Makes 2 servings

2 cups seedless green grapes

½ cup ice

½ frozen banana

½ cup baby kale

Combine grapes, ice, banana and kale in blender; blend until smooth.
Serve immediately.

CHERRY GREEN SMOOTHIE

Makes 2 servings

1 cup unsweetened almond milk

1½ cups frozen dark sweet cherries

¾ cup baby spinach

½ frozen banana

1 tablespoon ground flaxseed

2 teaspoons honey

Combine almond milk, cherries, spinach, banana, flaxseed and honey in blender; blend until smooth. Serve immediately.

GO GREEN SMOOTHIE

Makes 2 servings

½ cup unsweetened almond milk

2 cups baby spinach

1 cup seedless green grapes

1 avocado, pitted and peeled

1 cup ice cubes

2 teaspoons honey

Combine almond milk, spinach, grapes, avocado, ice and honey in blender; blend until smooth. Serve immediately.

TANGY APPLE KALE SMOOTHIE >

Makes 3 servings

1 cup water

2 Granny Smith apples, seeded and cut into chunks

2 cups baby kale

1 frozen banana

Combine water, apple, kale and banana in blender; blend until smooth. Serve immediately.

PEAR AVOCADO SMOOTHIE

Makes 2 servings

1 cup apple juice

1½ cups ice cubes

1 pear, seeded and cut into chunks

½ avocado, pitted and peeled

½ cup fresh mint leaves (about 6 sprigs)

2 tablespoons lime juice

Combine apple juice, ice, pear, avocado, mint and lime juice in blender; blend until smooth. Serve immediately.

PEACHES AND GREEN

Makes 1 serving

¾ cup unsweetened almond milk

1 cup packed stemmed spinach

1 cup frozen sliced peaches

1 cup ice cubes

2 tablespoons honey

½ teaspoon vanilla

Combine almond milk, spinach, peaches, ice, honey and vanilla in blender; blend until smooth. Serve immediately.

GREEN ISLANDER SMOOTHIE

Makes 2 servings

2 cups ice cubes

1 banana

1½ cups fresh pineapple chunks

1 cup packed stemmed spinach

1 cup packed stemmed kale

Combine ice, banana, pineapple, spinach and kale in blender; blend until smooth. Serve immediately.

GLORIOUSLY GREEN

Makes 2 servings

1 cup ice cubes

1½ cups honeydew chunks

2 kiwis, peeled and quartered

½ cup green seedless grapes

1 tablespoon honey

Combine ice, honeydew, kiwis, grapes and honey in blender; blend until smooth. Serve immediately.

GREENS GALORE

Makes 2 servings

¼ **cup water**

2 **small Granny Smith apples, seeded and cut into chunks**

1 **cup baby spinach**

⅓ **seedless cucumber, peeled and cut into chunks (4-inch piece)**

¼ **cup ice cubes**

⅓ **cup fresh mint leaves (about 3 sprigs)**

Combine water, apples, spinach, cucumber, ice and mint in blender; blend until smooth. Serve immediately.

GREEN CANTALOUPE QUENCHER

Makes 2 servings

2 cups cantaloupe chunks

1 cup frozen pineapple chunks

1 cup baby spinach

1 tablespoon ground flaxseed

Combine cantaloupe, pineapple, spinach and flaxseed in blender; blend until smooth. Serve immediately.

TROPICAL TREATS

··

TROPICAL STORM SMOOTHIE

Makes 2 servings

¼ **cup water**

1 **cup papaya chunks**

1 **cup frozen pineapple chunks**

½ **frozen banana**

1 **tablespoon lemon juice**

⅛ **teaspoon ground cinnamon**

Combine water, papaya, pineapple, banana, lemon juice and cinnamon in blender; blend until smooth. Serve immediately.

PINEAPPLE CRUSH

Makes 1 serving

½ **cup unsweetened coconut milk**

1½ **cups frozen pineapple chunks**

¼ **cup ice cubes**

½ **teaspoon vanilla**

Combine coconut milk, pineapple, ice and vanilla in blender; blend until smooth. Serve immediately.

STRAWBERRY BANANA COCONUT SMOOTHIE

Makes 3 servings

1¼ cups unsweetened coconut milk

2 cups frozen strawberries

1 banana

¼ cup ice cubes

1 tablespoon honey

Combine coconut milk, strawberries, banana, ice and honey in blender; blend until smooth. Serve immediately.

TROPICAL SUNRISE

Makes 2 servings

⅓ **cup unsweetened coconut milk**

⅓ **cup orange juice**

1 **frozen banana**

1 **cup frozen mango chunks**

½ **cup fresh pineapple chunks**

Combine coconut milk, orange juice, banana, mango and pineapple in blender; blend until smooth. Serve immediately.

PAPAYA-PINEAPPLE SMOOTHIE >

Makes 2 servings

½ **cup pineapple juice**

2 **cups papaya chunks**

1 **cup frozen pineapple chunks**

1 **tablespoon lime juice**

1 **to 2 tablespoons honey***

*Increase honey to 2 tablespoons depending on sweetness of papaya.

Combine pineapple juice, papaya, pineapple, lime juice and honey in blender; blend until smooth. Serve immediately.

PIÑA COLADA SMOOTHIE

Makes 1 serving

¾ **cup unsweetened coconut milk**

¾ **cup frozen pineapple chunks**

½ **banana**

Combine coconut milk, pineapple and banana in blender; blend until smooth. Serve immediately.

ISLAND DELIGHT SMOOTHIE

Makes 2 servings

- 1 cup unsweetened almond milk
- 1 frozen banana
- ½ cup frozen mango chunks
- 1 tablespoon almond butter

Combine almond milk, banana, mango and almond butter in blender; blend until smooth. Serve immediately.

KIWI PINEAPPLE CREAM

Makes 2 servings

¾ **cup unsweetened coconut milk**

1½ **cups fresh pineapple chunks**

2 **kiwis, peeled and quartered**

Grated peel and juice of 1 lime

Combine coconut milk, pineapple, kiwis, lime peel and lime juice in blender; blend until smooth. Serve immediately.

KIWI CHAI SMOOTHIE: Add ¼ teaspoon vanilla, ⅛ teaspoon ground cardamom, ⅛ teaspoon ground cinnamon, ⅛ teaspoon ground ginger and a pinch of ground cloves to the mixture before blending.

TROPICAL BREEZE SMOOTHIE

Makes 2 servings

½ cup unsweetened coconut milk

1 cup frozen pineapple chunks

1 cup frozen mango chunks

1 tablespoon honey

Combine coconut milk, pineapple, mango and honey in blender; blend until smooth. Serve immediately.

REFRESHING GREEN SMOOTHIE >

Makes 1 serving

¾ **cup unsweetened coconut milk**

1 **cup baby spinach**

¾ **cup frozen pineapple chunks**

½ **teaspoon grated lemon peel**

Combine coconut milk, spinach, pineapple and lemon peel in blender; blend until smooth. Serve immediately.

TROPICAL MANGO TANGO

Makes 3 servings

1¼ **cups coconut water**

1½ **cups frozen mango chunks**

½ **cup frozen pineapple chunks**

½ **banana**

1 **teaspoon grated fresh ginger**

Combine coconut water, mango, pineapple, banana and ginger in blender; blend until smooth. Serve immediately.

CUBAN BATIDO

Makes 3 servings

¾ **cup unsweetened coconut milk**

½ **cup orange juice**

1½ **cups fresh pineapple chunks**

1 **cup ice cubes**

1 **tablespoon lime juice**

Combine coconut milk, orange juice, pineapple, ice and lime juice in blender; blend until smooth. Serve immediately.

NOTE: A batido is a popular Latin American drink made with water, milk, fruit and ice. It is similar in texture to a smoothie and literally means "beaten" in Portuguese.

KIWI MANGO MAGIC

Makes 2 servings

1 cup water

2 kiwis, peeled and quartered

¾ cup frozen pineapple chunks

¾ cup frozen mango chunks

⅓ cup fresh mint leaves (about 3 sprigs)

Combine water, kiwis, pineapple, mango and mint in blender; blend until smooth. Serve immediately.

SUPERFOOD SMOOTHIES

··

POMEGRANATE FRUIT FLING

Makes 2 servings

¼ cup water

1 navel orange, peeled and seeded

1 small pear, seeded and cut into chunks

½ cup pomegranate seeds

¼ cup ice cubes

Combine water, orange, pear, pomegranate seeds and ice in blender; blend until smooth. Serve immediately.

SPICED PUMPKIN BANANA SMOOTHIE

Makes 1 serving

½ **cup unsweetened almond milk**

½ **frozen banana**

½ **cup ice cubes**

½ **cup canned pumpkin**

1 **tablespoon honey**

1 **teaspoon ground flaxseed**

¼ **teaspoon ground cinnamon**

⅛ **teaspoon ground ginger**

Dash ground nutmeg

Combine almond milk, banana, ice, pumpkin, honey, flaxseed, cinnamon, ginger and nutmeg in blender; blend until smooth. Serve immediately.

AUTUMN CELEBRATION SMOOTHIE

Makes 2 servings

2 plums, pitted and cut into chunks

1 pear, seeded and cut into chunks

½ cup fresh or thawed frozen cranberries

¼ cup ice cubes

⅛ teaspoon ground ginger

⅛ teaspoon ground cinnamon

Combine plums, pear, cranberries, ice, ginger and cinnamon in blender; blend until smooth. Serve immediately.

BLACKBERRY LIME SMOOTHIE

Makes 1 serving

½ cup unsweetened coconut milk

1 cup fresh blackberries

2 ice cubes

1 tablespoon lime juice

2 teaspoons honey

½ teaspoon grated lime peel

Combine coconut milk, blackberries, ice, lime juice, honey and lime peel in blender; blend until smooth. Serve immediately.

SUPER SMOOTHIE >

Makes 1 serving

½ cup apple juice

1 cup packed stemmed kale

1 cup baby spinach

1 banana

1 cup ice cubes

Combine apple juice, kale, spinach, banana and ice in blender; blend until smooth. Serve immediately.

AVOCADO BANANA SMOOTHIE

Makes 1 serving

½ cup water

1 frozen banana

1 avocado, pitted and peeled

⅓ cup baby spinach

2 teaspoons honey

¼ teaspoon grated lemon peel

Combine ½ cup water, banana, avocado, spinach, honey and lemon peel in blender; blend until smooth. Add additional water, 1 tablespoon at at time, until desired consistency is reached. Serve immediately.

BEET AND BERRY BLAST

Makes 2 servings

¾ **cup orange juice**

¾ **cup canned sliced beets**

¾ **cup frozen mixed berries**

¾ **cup ice cubes**

1½ **tablespoons lemon juice**

1½ **tablespoons honey**

Combine orange juice, beets, berries, ice, lemon juice and honey in blender; blend until smooth. Serve immediately.

SUPER BLUE SMOOTHIE

Makes 2 servings

½ **cup pomegranate juice**

¼ **cup water**

¾ **cup frozen blueberries**

¾ **cup frozen blackberries**

½ **avocado, pitted and peeled**

2 **teaspoons honey**

Combine pomegranate juice, water, blueberries, blackberries, avocado and honey in blender; blend until smooth. Serve immediately.

SALAD BAR SMOOTHIE

Makes 1 serving

1½ **cups ice cubes**

½ **banana**

½ **cup fresh raspberries**

½ **cup sliced fresh strawberries**

½ **cup fresh blueberries**

½ **cup packed stemmed spinach**

Combine ice, banana, raspberries, strawberries, blueberries and spinach in blender; blend until smooth. Serve immediately.

CINNAMON SQUASH PEAR SMOOTHIE >

Makes 1 serving

1 pear, seeded and cut into chunks

¾ cup frozen cooked winter squash

1 teaspoon honey

¼ teaspoon ground cinnamon

Combine pear, squash, honey and cinnamon in blender; blend until smooth. Serve immediately.

BLUE KALE SMOOTHIE

Makes 2 servings

¼ cup unsweetened almond milk

1 cup packed stemmed kale

1 frozen banana

½ cup fresh blueberries

¼ cup ice cubes

Combine almond milk, kale, banana, blueberries and ice in blender; blend until smooth. Serve immediately.

CHERRY BERRY POMEGRANATE SMOOTHIE
Makes 2 servings

¾ cup water

1 cup frozen dark sweet cherries

½ cup frozen strawberries

½ cup pomegranate seeds

1 tablespoon chia seeds

1 teaspoon lemon juice

Combine water, cherries, strawberries, pomegranate seeds, chia seeds and lemon juice in blender; blend until smooth. Serve immediately.

GREEN GOODNESS

Makes 3 servings

2 pears, seeded and cut into chunks

2 cups baby kale

1 avocado, pitted and peeled

1 cup ice cubes

½ cup fresh mint leaves (about 6 sprigs)

Combine pears, kale, avocado, ice and mint in blender; blend until smooth. Serve immediately.

CHOCOLATE BLUEBERRY SHAKE

Makes 1 serving

¼ cup unsweetened almond milk

½ cup fresh blueberries

¼ cup ice cubes

2 teaspoons honey

½ teaspoon unsweetened cocoa powder

Combine almond milk, blueberries, ice, honey and cocoa in blender; blend until smooth. Serve immediately.

IMMUNITY BOOSTERS

....

CRAN-ORANGE RASPBERRY SMOOTHIE

Makes 2 servings

¼ **cup water**

2 **navel oranges, peeled and seeded**

½ **cup fresh or thawed frozen cranberries**

½ **cup frozen raspberries**

2 **teaspoons honey**

Combine water, oranges, cranberries, raspberries and honey in blender; blend until smooth. Serve immediately.

STRAWBERRY BASIL COOLER

Makes 2 servings

> 1 cup water
>
> 1¼ cups frozen strawberries
>
> ½ cup ice cubes
>
> ¼ cup fresh basil leaves
>
> 2 teaspoons lemon juice
>
> 2 teaspoons honey

Combine water, strawberries, ice, basil, lemon juice and honey in blender; blend until smooth. Serve immediately.

BLUEBERRY PEACH BLISS

Makes 2 servings

1¼ cups water

1 cup frozen blueberries

1 cup frozen sliced peaches

1 tablespoon lemon juice

2 teaspoons honey

½ teaspoon grated fresh ginger

Combine water, blueberries, peaches, lemon juice, honey and ginger in blender; blend until smooth. Serve immediately.

BERRY CRANBERRY BLAST

Makes 2 servings

1 cup water

1 cup frozen mixed berries

½ cup fresh or thawed frozen cranberries

½ avocado, pitted and peeled

1 tablespoon honey

½ teaspoon grated fresh ginger

Combine water, mixed berries, cranberries, avocado, honey and ginger in blender; blend until smooth. Serve immediately.

BLUEBERRY APPLE BOOSTER

Makes 2 servings

½ **cup apple juice**

1½ **cups frozen blueberries**

1 **Granny Smith apple, seeded and cut into chunks**

⅛ **teaspoon ground allspice**

Combine apple juice, blueberries, apple and allspice in blender; blend until smooth. Serve immediately.

MIXED BERRY BLEND >

Makes 2 servings

1 cup apple juice

1½ cups sliced fresh strawberries

1 cup fresh blueberries

½ cup fresh raspberries

½ cup ice cubes

Combine apple juice, strawberries, blueberries, raspberries and ice in blender; blend until smooth. Serve immediately.

FROZEN WATERMELON WHIP

Makes 2 servings

1 cup brewed lemon herbal tea, at room temperature

1¾ cups ice cubes

1½ cups seedless watermelon chunks

Combine tea, ice and watermelon in blender; blend until smooth. Serve immediately.

SUPER C SMOOTHIE

Makes 3 servings

⅔ cup water

2 navel oranges, peeled and seeded

2 cups baby kale

2 cups frozen blackberries

1 avocado, pitted and peeled

2 tablespoons honey

Combine water, oranges, kale, blackberries, avocado and honey in blender; blend until smooth. Serve immediately.

SPA SMOOTHIE

Makes 3 servings

1 cup diced peeled cucumber

1 cup cantaloupe chunks

1 cup sliced fresh strawberries

1 cup ice cubes

Grated peel and juice of 2 lemons

2 tablespoons honey

Combine cucumber, cantaloupe, strawberries, ice, lemon peel, lemon juice and honey in blender; blend until smooth. Serve immediately.

GRAPE STRAWBERRY SUNSET

Makes 2 servings

½ cup water

1 sweet red apple, seeded and cut into chunks

1 cup frozen red seedless grapes

1 cup frozen strawberries

1 teaspoon lemon juice

Combine water, apple, grapes, strawberries and lemon juice in blender; blend until smooth. Serve immediately.

CHERRY ALMOND SMOOTHIE

Makes 2 servings

½ **cup unsweetened almond milk**

1½ **cups frozen dark sweet cherries**

½ **banana**

2 **teaspoons almond butter**

⅛ **teaspoon ground cinnamon**

Combine almond milk, cherries, banana, almond butter and cinnamon in blender; blend until smooth. Serve immediately.

ORANGE APRICOT SUNSHINE

Makes 2 servings

½ **cup dried apricots**

¾ **cup water**

 1 **navel orange, peeled and seeded**

½ **cup frozen mango chunks**

½ **teaspoon grated fresh ginger**

1. Place apricots in small bowl; cover with hot water. Let stand 10 minutes; drain.

2. Combine water, orange, mango, apricots and ginger in blender; blend until smooth. Serve immediately.

BERRY TANGERINE DREAM

Makes 3 servings

½ cup water

2 tangerines, peeled and seeded

2 cups frozen mixed berries

1 cup fresh pineapple chunks

2 teaspoons honey

Combine water, tangerines, mixed berries, pineapple and honey in blender; blend until smooth. Serve immediately.

ENERGIZING SMOOTHIES

··

BERRY MOJITO SMOOTHIE
Makes 2 servings

1¼ cups water

1 cup frozen strawberries

½ cup frozen raspberries

1 tablespoon lime juice

1 tablespoon honey

½ cup fresh mint leaves (about 6 sprigs)

Combine water, strawberries, raspberries, lime juice, honey and mint in blender; blend until smooth. Serve immediately.

BLUEBERRY CHERRY BLEND

Makes 2 servings

¾ **cup water**

¾ **cup frozen blueberries**

¾ **cup frozen dark sweet cherries**

½ **avocado, pitted and peeled**

1 **tablespoon lemon juice**

1 **teaspoon ground flaxseed**

Combine water, blueberries, cherries, avocado, lemon juice and flaxseed in blender; blend until smooth. Serve immediately.

LEMON STRAWBERRY SMOOTHIE

Makes 1 serving

¾ cup unsweetened almond milk

1 cup sliced fresh strawberries

¼ cup ice cubes

1 tablespoon honey

1 tablespoon lemon juice

1 teaspoon grated lemon peel

Combine almond milk, strawberries, ice, honey, lemon juice and lemon peel in blender; blend until smooth. Serve immediately.

KIWI GREEN DREAM

Makes 2 servings

¾ **cup water**

2 **kiwis, peeled and quartered**

½ **cup frozen pineapple chunks**

½ **avocado, pitted and peeled**

1 **tablespoon chia seeds**

Combine water, kiwis, pineapple, avocado and chia seeds in blender; blend until smooth. Serve immediately.

PURPLE PICK-ME-UP >

Makes 2 servings

¼ cup water

1 navel orange, peeled and seeded

1 cup frozen blueberries

4 medjool dates, pitted

Combine water, orange, blueberries and dates in blender; blend until smooth. Serve immediately.

CHEERY CHERRY SMOOTHIE

Makes 2 servings

1 cup unsweetened coconut milk

1 cup frozen sliced peaches

½ cup frozen dark sweet cherries

2 teaspoons lemon juice

Dash ground allspice

Combine coconut milk, peaches, cherries, lemon juice and allspice in blender; blend until smooth. Serve immediately.

SWEET BEET TREAT

Makes 2 servings

¼ **cup water**

2 medium carrots, cut into chunks (about 4 ounces)

1 medium beet, peeled and cut into chunks

1 large sweet red apple, seeded and cut into chunks

¼ **cup ice cubes**

1 tablespoon lemon juice

Combine water, carrots, beet, apple, ice and lemon juice in blender; blend until smooth. Serve immediately.

RASPBERRY LEMON BRAIN FREEZE

Makes 2 servings

½ **cup water**

⅓ **cup lemon juice (about 2 lemons)**

1 **cup ice cubes**

¾ **cup frozen raspberries**

3 **tablespoons honey**

Combine water, lemon juice, ice, raspberries and honey in blender; blend until smooth. Serve immediately.

GREEN POWER SMOOTHIE

Makes 3 servings

½ cup coconut water or water

2 cups packed stemmed spinach

1 cup fresh pineapple chunks

1 cup frozen mango chunks

½ frozen banana

Combine coconut water, spinach, pineapple, mango and banana in blender; blend until smooth. Serve immediately.

REFRESH SMOOTHIE >

Makes 1 serving

½ cucumber, peeled, seeded and cut into chunks

1 cup frozen mixed berries

¼ cup ice cubes

1 tablespoon honey

Grated peel and juice of 1 lime

Combine cucumber, mixed berries, ice, honey, lime peel and lime juice in blender; blend until smooth. Serve immediately.

ENERGY SMOOTHIE

Makes 2 servings

½ cup unsweetened almond milk

1½ cups sliced fresh strawberries

1 frozen banana

2 tablespoons lemon juice

Combine almond milk, strawberries, banana and lemon juice in blender; blend until smooth. Serve immediately.

PUMPKIN POWER SMOOTHIE

Makes 1 serving

⅓ cup water

1 sweet red apple, seeded and cut into chunks

½ frozen banana

½ cup ice cubes

½ cup canned pumpkin

1 tablespoon lemon juice

1 tablespoon ground flaxseed

1 teaspoon honey

Dash ground nutmeg

Combine water, apple, banana, ice, pumpkin, lemon juice, flaxseed, honey and nutmeg in blender; blend until smooth. Serve immediately.

GREEN PINEAPPLE PICK-ME-UP

Makes 1 serving

½ cup frozen pineapple chunks

½ avocado, pitted and peeled

1 cup baby kale

2 tablespoons water

1 tablespoon lime juice

1 teaspoon honey

Combine pineapple, avocado, kale, water, lime juice and honey in blender; blend until smooth. Serve immediately.

CRANBERRY APPLE CRUSH

Makes 1 serving

¼ **cup water**

 1 **sweet red apple, seeded and cut into chunks**

½ **cup fresh or thawed frozen cranberries**

½ **frozen banana**

 2 **teaspoons honey**

⅛ **teaspoon ground cinnamon**

Combine water, apple, cranberries, banana, honey and cinnamon in blender; blend until smooth. Serve immediately.

RAPID REFRESHERS

. . . .

RASPBERRY PEAR REFRESHER

Makes 2 servings

¾ **cup water**

1 **pear, seeded and cut into chunks**

1 **clementine, peeled**

1 **cup frozen raspberries**

Combine water, pear, clementine and raspberries in blender; blend until smooth. Serve immediately.

CREAMY MANGO SMOOTHIE

Makes 3 servings

1½ cups unsweetened coconut milk

2 cups frozen mango chunks

1 orange, peeled and seeded

¾ teaspoon vanilla

Combine coconut milk, mango, orange and vanilla in blender; blend until smooth. Serve immediately.

GRAPE CHERRY SMOOTHIE

Makes 2 servings

1 cup seedless red grapes

1 navel orange, peeled and seeded

½ cup frozen dark sweet cherries

¼ cup ice cubes

Combine grapes, orange, cherries and ice in blender; blend until smooth. Serve immediately.

SPEEDY RASPBERRY SMOOTHIE >

Makes 2 servings

1 cup unsweetened almond milk

2 cups frozen raspberries

½ avocado, pitted and peeled

2 tablespoons lemon juice

1 tablespoon honey

Combine almond milk, raspberries, avocado, lemon juice and honey in blender; blend until smooth. Serve immediately.

MANGOLICIOUS BANANA SMOOTHIE

Makes 2 servings

1 cup orange juice

1¼ cups frozen mango chunks

1 banana

Combine orange juice, mango and banana in blender; blend until smooth. Serve immediately.

LEMON-LIME WATERMELON AGUA FRESCA

Makes 3 servings

5 cups seedless watermelon chunks

½ cup ice water

Grated peel and juice of 1 lemon

Grated peel and juice of 1 lime

1. Combine watermelon, water, lemon peel and juice and lime peel and juice in blender; blend until smooth.

2. Serve immediately over ice or refrigerate until ready to serve.

CHOCOLATE RASPBERRY SMOOTHIE

Makes 1 serving

½ **cup unsweetened almond milk**

1 **cup frozen raspberries**

1 **tablespoon unsweetened cocoa powder**

1 **teaspoon honey**

Combine almond milk, raspberries, cocoa and honey in blender; blend until smooth. Serve immediately.

PLUM CHERRY SMOOTHIE

Makes 1 serving

1 plum, pitted and cut into chunks

1 cup frozen dark sweet cherries

½ frozen banana

Combine plum, cherries and banana in blender; blend until smooth. Serve immediately.

STRAWBERRY CLEMENTINE SMOOTHIE >

Makes 2 servings

⅓ **cup water**

2 **cups frozen strawberries, slightly thawed**

1 **frozen banana**

2 **clementines, peeled**

Combine water, strawberries, banana and clementines in blender; blend until smooth. Serve immediately.

PALEO PEACH COCONUT SMOOTHIE

Makes 2 servings

1 **cup unsweetened coconut milk**

1½ **cups frozen sliced peaches**

¼ **teaspoon grated lemon peel**

Combine coconut milk, peaches and lemon peel in blender; blend until smooth. Serve immediately.

RASPBERRY CHERRY SMOOTHIE

Makes 2 servings

⅔ cup apple juice

1 cup frozen raspberries

1 cup frozen dark sweet cherries, slightly thawed

½ avocado, pitted and peeled

Combine apple juice, raspberries, cherries and avocado in blender; blend until smooth. Serve immediately.

PEACH VANILLA SMOOTHIE

Makes 1 serving

½ cup unsweetened almond milk

1 cup frozen sliced peaches

½ cup ice cubes

2 teaspoons honey

½ teaspoon vanilla

Combine almond milk, peaches, ice, honey and vanilla in blender; blend until smooth. Serve immediately.

METRIC CONVERSION CHART

VOLUME MEASUREMENTS (dry)

1/8 teaspoon = 0.5 mL
1/4 teaspoon = 1 mL
1/2 teaspoon = 2 mL
3/4 teaspoon = 4 mL
1 teaspoon = 5 mL
1 tablespoon = 15 mL
2 tablespoons = 30 mL
1/4 cup = 60 mL
1/3 cup = 75 mL
1/2 cup = 125 mL
2/3 cup = 150 mL
3/4 cup = 175 mL
1 cup = 250 mL
2 cups = 1 pint = 500 mL
3 cups = 750 mL
4 cups = 1 quart = 1 L

VOLUME MEASUREMENTS (fluid)

1 fluid ounce (2 tablespoons) = 30 mL
4 fluid ounces (1/2 cup) = 125 mL
8 fluid ounces (1 cup) = 250 mL
12 fluid ounces (1 1/2 cups) = 375 mL
16 fluid ounces (2 cups) = 500 mL

WEIGHTS (mass)

1/2 ounce = 15 g
1 ounce = 30 g
3 ounces = 90 g
4 ounces = 120 g
8 ounces = 225 g
10 ounces = 285 g
12 ounces = 360 g
16 ounces = 1 pound = 450 g

DIMENSIONS

1/16 inch = 2 mm
1/8 inch = 3 mm
1/4 inch = 6 mm
1/2 inch = 1.5 cm
3/4 inch = 2 cm
1 inch = 2.5 cm

OVEN TEMPERATURES

250°F = 120°C
275°F = 140°C
300°F = 150°C
325°F = 160°C
350°F = 180°C
375°F = 190°C
400°F = 200°C
425°F = 220°C
450°F = 230°C

BAKING PAN SIZES

Utensil	Size in Inches/Quarts	Metric Volume	Size in Centimeters
Baking or Cake Pan (square or rectangular)	8×8×2	2 L	20×20×5
	9×9×2	2.5 L	23×23×5
	12×8×2	3 L	30×20×5
	13×9×2	3.5 L	33×23×5
Loaf Pan	8×4×3	1.5 L	20×10×7
	9×5×3	2 L	23×13×7
Round Layer Cake Pan	8×1½	1.2 L	20×4
	9×1½	1.5 L	23×4
Pie Plate	8×1¼	750 mL	20×3
	9×1¼	1 L	23×3
Baking Dish or Casserole	1 quart	1 L	—
	1½ quart	1.5 L	—
	2 quart	2 L	—